Spanish for Little Boys

A beginning Spanish workbook
for little boys

Written by: Yvonne Crawford
Illustrations by: Angelique Lackey

www.languageforlittlelearners.com

About this workbook

All people learn a foreign language best when they are properly motivated. This workbook is designed to target the obsessions of little boys: cars, trains, bugs, and more. You and your son will open the door to the Spanish language while coloring trains, playing memory games with different types of bugs and racing his favorite toy car down an exciting race track full of obstacles.

This workbook is created especially for parents who do not have any prior knowledge of Spanish. You and your son can embark on a journey of learning a foreign language together. Everything you need is inside this workbook, including a pronunciation guide, dictionary and teaching hints.

Every lesson will consist of a list of vocabulary words with pictures, three activities your son can do in the workbook with your guidance and two activities you can do together without the workbook for further practice. Each new word that is introduced will have its pronunciation next to it.

In the appendix there is a progress sheet for your child. When you and your child finish a lesson, turn to page 68 and have your child color a stepping stone. This will help your child to see, and take pride in his progress.

Do not put stress on your son to have perfect pronunciation or to remember every single word. If he forgets a word, simply repeat it and then use it in a sentence a few times; eventually he will catch on. It is important for him (and you) to have a positive first experience with learning a foreign language. It will encourage him to continue in the future with more language studies.

If your son is learning quickly, have him try the challenges that are placed throughout the workbook. They are designed for children who need and desire more language learning.

Table of Contents

Lección 1

Hello Bugs!

Vocabulary:

la abeja *lah-ah-**bay**-hah*
bee

la mariquita
*lah-mah-ree-**kee**-tah*
ladybug

la mariposa
*lah-mah-ree-**poh**-sah*
butterfly

la hormiga *lah-ohr-**mee**-gah*
ant

la araña *lah-ah-**rah**-nyah*
spider

Fun Phrases:

hola	**oh**-la	hello
adiós	a-dee-**ohs**	good-bye
hasta luego	**ahs**-tah-loo-**ay**-goh	see you later

Teaching Tips:

- Throughout the day, point out the bugs that you see and ask your child what they are called in Spanish. Before you know it your child will be making sentences like '¡Look, there's a *mariposa*!'

- Some letters sound different in Spanish than they do in English. Refer to each word's pronunciation guide to see the proper pronunciation.

- Usually for Spanish words which end in vowels, the stress is put on the 2nd to last syllable. If the word ends with a consonant, then the stress is put on the final syllable. In this workbook, the stressed syllable is bolded to aid teaching.

Actividad Uno

¡Hola! My name is Pedro. I am an iguana and I love to play games. Can you match the picture of each bug to its correct name?

la mariposa

la araña

la abeja

Actividad Dos

Now you can greet each of my bug friends in Spanish! For each picture above greet the bug, say '¡Hola!', then say the name of the bug.

Actividad Tres

Can you help me match the baby bugs with their mothers? Every time you match two, make sure you say their names in Spanish!

Actividad Cuatro

A Home for Bugs

What you will need:

a shoe box or jar
crayons
scissors
construction paper
tape or glue

What to do:

1. Take a shoe box or jar to create a bug house. Decorate your bug house with construction paper and crayons. You can even draw some bugs of your own on the outside, so the bugs will feel right at home. Make sure to cut some holes in the box, so the bugs can breathe.
2. With your parent, take your bug home to your backyard or to a park and find some bugs. Every time you find a bug, say its name in Spanish.

Actividad Cinco

Rock Bugs

What you will need:

a few flat rocks
paint
a paintbrush

What to do:

1. Paint each of the 5 bugs listed in this lesson on the rocks. As you paint them make sure you repeat their names in Spanish.
2. After letting your rock bugs dry, ask a parent to hide them in your backyard, sand pit, or anywhere. Then, as you find each bug, tell your parent which bug you found in Spanish.

Lección 2
Polite Pets

Pedro's Pet Shop

el perro *ehl-pehr-roh*
dog

el pez *ehl-pays*
fish

el conejo
ehl-coh-nay-hoh
rabbit

el gato
ehl-gah-toh
cat

el pájaro
ehl-pah-hah-roh
bird

Fun Phrases:

¿Cómo estás?	*koh*-moh-eh-*stahs*	How are you?
estoy bien	eh-*stoy*-bee-*in*	I'm well.
estoy mal	eh-*stoy*-mahl	I'm bad.
así así	ah-*see*-ah-*see*	so-so
gracias	*grah*-see-ahs	thank you
de nada	day-*nah*-dah	you're welcome
por favor	pohr-fay-*vohr*	please

Teaching Tips:

- In Spanish when you say a sentence like, 'I'm well,' you do not need to say 'I'. Instead you drop 'I' (Yo).

    Yo estoy bien —> Estoy bien.

- Encourage your child to color all of the vocabulary page pictures. You can use this time to reinforce the new words. You and your child can repeat each word as he colors its corresponding picture.

- Remember to watch for signs that your child needs to take a break. You can always start where you left off tomorrow!

- Unlike in English, in Spanish each sound is specifically spoken, so don't be afraid to really enunciate the sounds.

Actividad Uno

Come and meet my friends! Say *¡hola!* to each animal. Next, draw a line from the animal to its favorite food. Your mom or dad can pretend to be the animal and say *gracias* for "thank you." You can reply *de nada* for "you're welcome" to each animal.

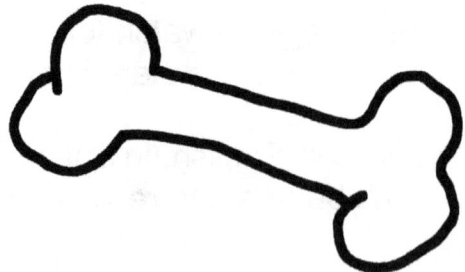

Actividad Dos

Oh no, the pets in the pictures have no mouths! Will you draw mouths for each animal? Make two of the faces happy, one of the faces sad and one of the faces so-so. Then, when you are finished, ask the animal *¿Cómo estás?* Then, pretend to be the animal and reply with *Estoy bien*, *Estoy mal* or *así así*. Use the following rabbits as an example.

Actividad Tres

This is Pedro's favorite story about his visit to a pet store to pick out a pet. Your mom or dad can read the story to you, and whenever you see a picture in the story, say the word in Spanish.

| Pedro | el perro | el conejo | el gato | el pez | el pájaro |

Pedro's Trip to the Pet Store

One day  decided that he wanted a pet. He asked his mom if

he could have one. She said, "Okay , you may have one.

Let's go to the pet store and pick one out." They went to the pet store

and the first animal they saw was a big  .  jumped up

and down and said "I want a ". His mom replied " I'm sorry

 ,  is too big for our house, you need something

smaller.". He immediately found another pet that he liked, 'Mom I would

like this  , por favor. His mom looked at the  and imagined

it tweeting all night. "I'm sorry, that  is too loud, find a pet that is

quieter.  looked and looked, then he saw a  .

"I want this  . He's so quiet,"  said.

16

Mom looked at the mess that the 🐰 had made in his cage and she said "I'm sorry dear, he is too messy. You need to find a pet that is cleaner'. 🦎 saw a 🐱 licking himself and he said, "A Mom? I think they are very clean."Oh 🦎 ", Mom said sadly, "I love cats, but the fur makes me sneeze, ah ah ah chooo!" 🦎 was about to give up when he saw a 🐟 swimming around in a bowl. He thought to himself, before he told his mom, 'The 🐟 is not too big like a 🐕 It does not make too much noise, like a 🐤 It is not too messy, like a 🐰 . It does not have fur that makes mom sneeze, like a 🐱 Maybe this pet might work. "Mom," 🦎 asked tentatively, "Can I have a 🐟 ?' 'Of course", mom replied. Pedro and his mom went home with his new pet 🐟 .

Fin - The End

Teaching Tips:

- You can repeat this story several times over the course of this book to reinforce the names of animals in Spanish.

Actividad Cuatro

Be Polite

Throughout the day, use your Spanish! When you would like something from your mom or dad, say *por favor*. The most important word is *gracias* for thank you. Also, there is *de nada* for you're welcome. Every time you say one of these polite expressions today, you can come back to this workbook and record it on this page. Color a star for each time you use one of your new Spanish phrases.

por favor   *gracias*   *de nada*

☆ ☆ ☆ ☆ ☆ ☆ ☆ ☆ ☆

Actividad Cinco

Faces

What you will need:
construction paper
markers/crayons
scissors

What to do:
1. With your mom's or dad's help, cut out three big circles.
2. Draw a face in each circle. Make sure to include eyes, a nose, ears, and hair on each of the three circles.
3. Now, draw a smiley mouth on one circle, a frown on one circle and a so-so face on the last circle. As you are drawing the mouths, repeat the phrases in Spanish *estoy bien*, *estoy mal* and *así así*.
4. Take a large piece of construction paper, tape all of the faces onto it, and hang it on the fridge.
5. Throughout the day, go to the faces and practice saying "How are you?" in Spanish by saying *¿Cómo estás?,* then you can point to the face that shows how you feel, and say the phrase in Spanish.

Lección 3

Truckin' through Numbers

Vocabulary:

el coche *ehl-**koh**-chay*
car

el camión *ehl-cah-mee-**ohn***
truck

la motocicleta
*lah-moh-toh-see-**klay**-tah*
motorcycle

la bicicleta
*lah-bee-see-**clay**-tah*
bicycle

1 **uno** *oo-noh*
one

2 **dos** *dohs*
two

3 **tres** *trays*
three

4 **cuatro** *koo-aht-troh*
four

5 **cinco** *seen-koh*
five

Teaching Tips:

- In order to reinforce learning the numbers, use the Spanish numbers throughout the day. Whenever your child says a number in English, ask them to say it in Spanish as well.

- When a word ends with a vowel, add an 's' to the end of a noun to make it plural.
    - una motocicleta - one motorcycle
    - dos motocicletas - two motorcycles

Actividad Uno

Count the different vehicles in Spanish, then write the number in the box.

Actividad Dos

This old *camión* needs some new tires. Circle the stack with *cuatro* tires.

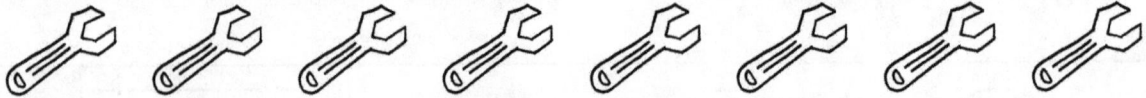

Challenge:

Take a few toasted oat cereal rings and stack the "tires" in amounts ranging from one to five. Count the number of tires in each stack in Spanish.

Actividad Tres

Follow the path of each vehicle and find out which one leads to me!

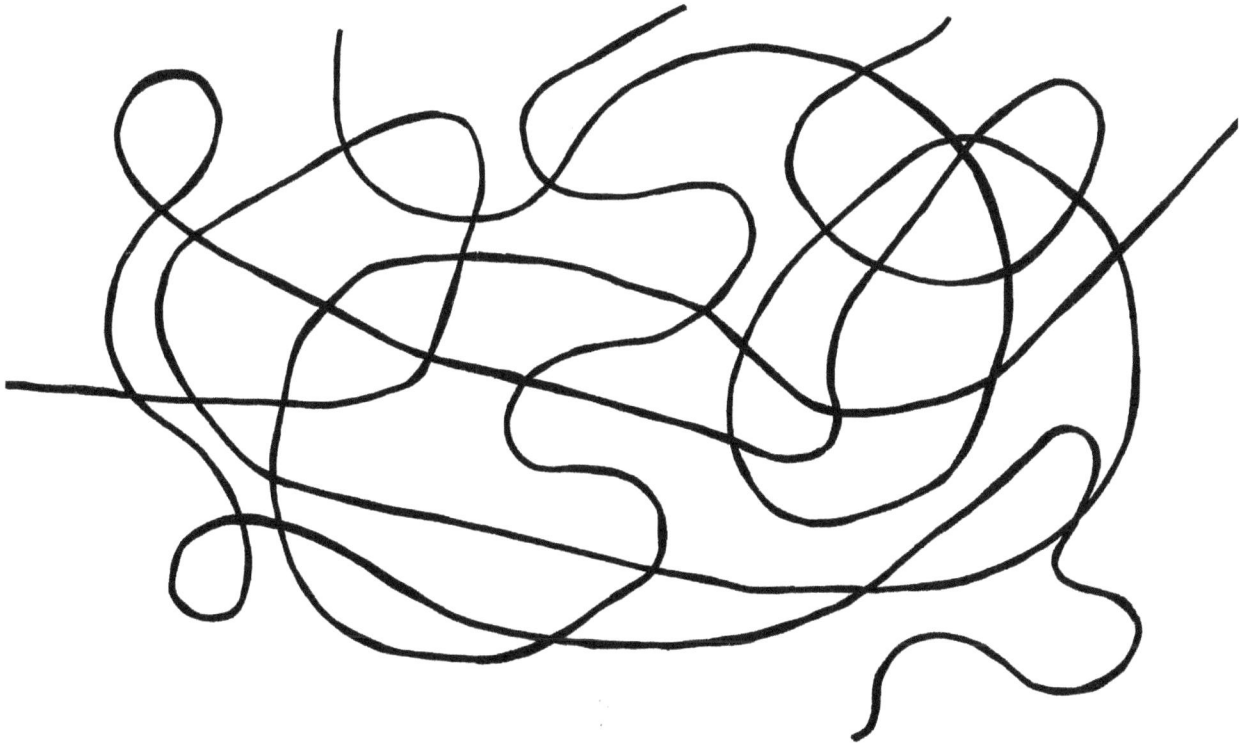

Actividad Cuatro

Counting Cars

Gather five of your toy *coches* and *camións*, then count them. Say phrases like: *cinco coches* and *dos camiónes* as you play with them. You can also practice being polite by sharing your cars with your parents. When you give them a car, they can say *gracias* and you can reply *de nada*.

Actividad Cinco

Car Scrapbook

What you will need:
old magazines or old car brochures
newspaper advertisements
construction paper
glue
scissors
a hole punch
yarn
crayons

What to do:
1. Look through the magazines and brochures. Find pictures of cars and trucks that you like.
2. Repeat their names in Spanish as you cut them out.
3. Fold a piece of construction paper in half and glue your pictures on all parts of the paper.
4. After you finish finding cars and trucks for your scrapbook, have your parents help you punch holes in it on one side, thread a piece of yarn through the holes, and then tie the yarn in order to bind your book.
5. Finally, decorate your book by coloring it.

Lección 4

Colors

Vocabulary:

verde *vehrr-day*
green

azul *ah-sool*
blue

rojo *roh-hoh*
red

Amarillo
ah-mah-ree-yoh
yellow

negro *nay-groh*
black

blanco *blahn-koh*
white

anaranjado
ah-nah-rahn-hah-doh
orange

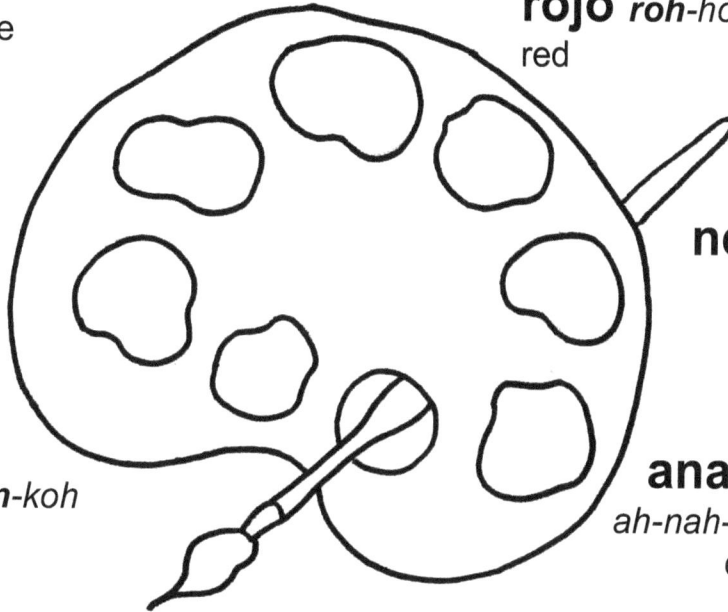

Fun Phrases:

me llamo	*meh-yah-moh*	my name is
¿Cómo te llamas?	*koh-moh-tay-yah-mahs*	What is your name?
y	*ee*	and

Teaching tips:
- Most adjectives in Spanish follow the noun, for example:
    el coche azul - the blue car
    el camión verde - the green truck

Challenge:
- You can also ask this question to your child to reinforce colors.
    ¿Cuál color? *koo-ahl-koo-lohr* - which color?

Actividad Uno

Let's color my animal friends. Use the key to color the different animals.

el pájaro	verde
el perro	azul
el gato	anaranjado
el pez	negro
el conejo	amarillo

Actividad Dos

Color the vehicles below different colors and say their names in Spanish.

Challenge:

Use *hay,* which means "there is/there are" to explain to your parents what is happening in this picture.

Hay un coche rojo. - There is a red car.
Hay un camión azul. - There is a blue truck.

Actividad Tres

Use the frame below and draw a picture of yourself. Write your name at the bottom after *Me llamo* and show your mom and dad that you can say "My name is…" in Spanish.

Me llamo _____.

Actividad Cuatro

Rainbow Rice

What you will need:

rice

food coloring

a plastic container with a lid

What to do:

1. Take the bag of rice and pour it into the plastic container
2. Spread the rice evenly in the container.
3. Pick up each bottle of food coloring, and practice saying the names of the colors in Spanish.
4. With your mom's or dad's help, pour the different colors of food coloring into separate sections of the rice. Try not to mix them up so that you will have nice vibrant colors.
5. Allow the rice to dry for at least 1 hour.
6. Now, you can play with your special new colored rice. As you play you can talk about the different colors. You can also drive your toy cars through it and make mountains of colored rice for them to climb over. Have fun with it!

Actividad Cinco

Hello Friends

What you will need:

Your favorite toys with names (if they don't have names, now may be the time to name them) - trains, stuffed animals, anything…

What to do:

1. Line up all of your toys and ask the first toy "¿Cómo te llamas?" which means "What is your name?"
2. Then, reply for your toy (in a different voice) "Me llamo…"
3. Continue with the rest of your toys doing the same thing.

Lección 5
Flying with More Numbers

Vocabulary:

la cometa
*lah-coh-**may**-tah*
kite

el cohete
*ehl-coh-**ay**-tay*
rocket

el globo aerostático
*ehl-**gloh**-boh-ah-ay-rohs-**tah**-tee-koh*
hot air balloon

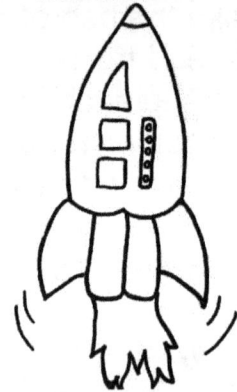

el helicóptero
*ehl-ay-lee-**cohp**-tay-roh*
helicopter

el avión
*ehl-ah-vee-**ohn**
airplane

seis *say-ees* **6**
six

siete *see-**eh**-tay* **7**
seven

ocho *oh-choh* **8**
eight

nueve *noo-**ay**-vay* **9**
nine

diez *dee-ehs* **10**
ten

Actividad Uno

¡Hola! Look at the picture below. Can you help me find the *avión, cometa, globo aerostático, cohete,* and *helicóptero*? Each time you find one, use your Spanish. Say 'I see a …' then the name in Spanish. When you find one, color it! And at the end you can count all of the high flyers that you have colored!

Actividad Dos

Pedro has drawn a picture for you, but he has forgotten to connect some of the dots. Use your crayon and connect all of the dots to finish his picture. As you connect the dots say each number in Spanish!

1

10

3

2

4

5

8   7

6

9

Actividad Tres

Count the pictures below in Spanish, and then circle the correct number.

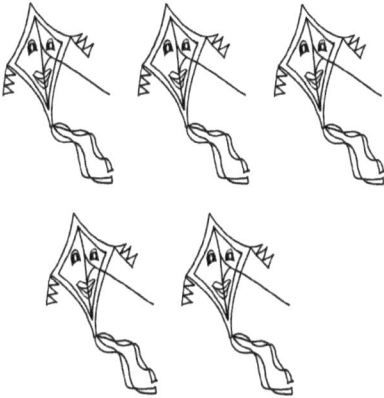

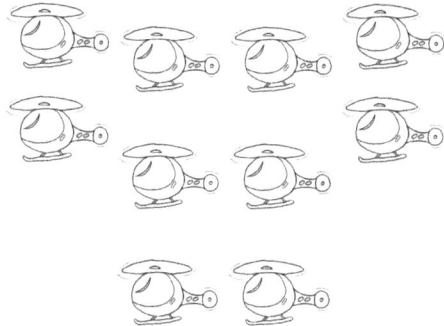

5	6	7

8	10	9

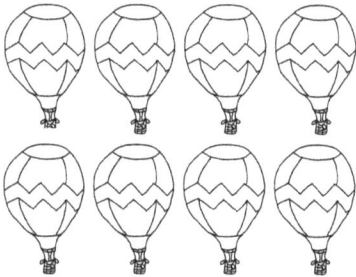

7	9	8

7	6	5

Challenge:

Start a collection of objects! Brainstorm with your parent about different things that could be in your collection (toy cars, rocks, sea shells, pencils, stamps, postcards). After gathering the objects for your collection, count the number of items in your collection in Spanish.

Actividad Cuatro

To the Moon...

What you will need:

construction paper
empty toilet paper rolls
crayons or markers
tape or glue
scissors

What to do:

1. Imagine you are going to the moon. What kind of spaceship would you like to take you there?
2. Using all of the supplies, create a spaceship from your imagination.
3. After you have completed your spaceship, now you can launch it. Say your countdown in Spanish 5-4-3-2-1... *¡Que tengas un buen viaje!* Have a good trip!

Actividad Cinco

Kites!

What you will need:

construction paper
crayons
yarn
scissors
glue

What to do:

1. Using one piece of construction paper, cut out a diamond shape to make your kite.
2. Decorate your kite by coloring different shapes and designs.
3. Cut a piece of yarn for the tail of your kite and glue it to your kite.
4. Cut small pieces of construction paper to be the ribbons on the tail of your kite. Then, attach the tail to the kite with glue.
5. After waiting for your kite to dry, hang your kite from the ceiling or high on the wall. When you see it, say *"¡la cometa!"*

Lección 6

Robots

Vocabulary:

el robot *ehl-roh-boht*
robot

la cabeza
lah-kah-bay-sah
head

la mano
lah-mah-noh
hand

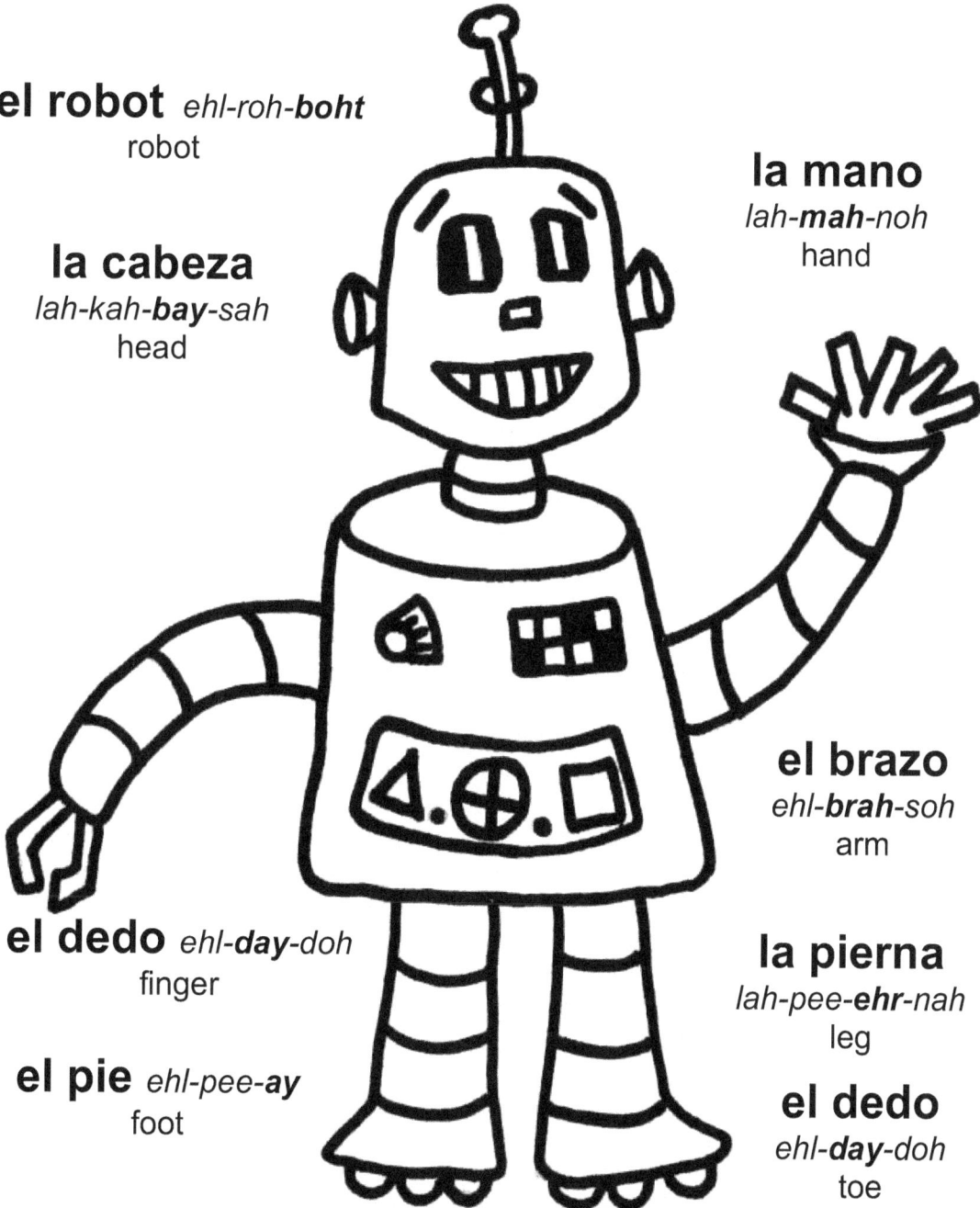

el brazo
ehl-brah-soh
arm

el dedo *ehl-day-doh*
finger

el pie *ehl-pee-ay*
foot

la pierna
lah-pee-ehr-nah
leg

el dedo
ehl-day-doh
toe

Fun Phrases:

tengo	*tayn*-goh	I have
tienes	tee-*ehn*-ehs	you have

Teaching Tips:

- It's important to review previous lessons to make sure your child remembers other words he has learned.

Challenge:

- Use this question word to help your child practice numbers in Spanish:

cuántos	*quahn*-tohs	how many

Actividad Uno

Let's build a robot! Below are the bodies and heads of two robots, use your crayons to draw *piernas, manos, dedos,* and all other parts of the robot. As you draw each body part, say the word in Spanish.

Actividad Dos

Look at the different pictures of robots. In each row find the one robot that is different from the other two and tell your parent which body part is different, in Spanish.

Actividad Tres

Say these words in Spanish and then draw a line from each word to its matching picture.

la pierna   el brazo   el dedo   la cabeza

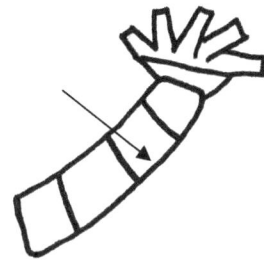

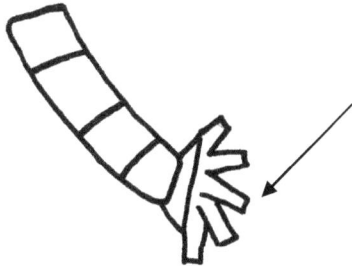

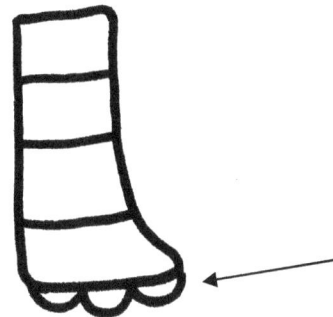

Challenge:

Sing and act out the "Hokey Pokey" song with your child using the Spanish term for each body part focused on in this lesson. You can sing the song in English and say the body parts in Spanish. For example: "You put your right *pierna* in. You put your right *pierna* out. You put your right *pierna* in and you shake it all about. You do the hokey pokey and you turn yourself around. That's what it's all about!"

Actividad Cuatro

Making Robots

What you will need:

Modeling clay

What to do:

1. Make robot body parts together with your mom or dad. As you finish making each body part say the name and color of it in Spanish. For example: *la cabeza roja*
2. Build some robots. After you have built a few robots, you can pretend to be a robot and speak to your mom or dad. You can say things like *¡Hola!* and *¿Cómo estás?*

Challenge:

You can also describe what you see:

veo	*vay-oh*	I see

Veo una pierna roja. I see a red leg.

Actividad Cinco

A Paper Me

What you will need:

freezer paper
crayons
scissors

What to do:

1. Roll out a big sheet of freezer paper on the floor - about the size of yourself.
2. Have your mom or dad trace your body onto the paper.
3. Draw and color your hair, face and clothes.
4. Ask your mom or dad to help cut out your picture of yourself and then hang it on a wall or door.
5. Point to all of your body parts on the picture and say their names in Spanish.

Lección 7

All Aboard!

Vocabulary:

la locomotora
lah-loh-koh-moh-toh-rah
engine

la vagoneta
lah-vah-gohn-nay-tah
tender

el vagón de pasajero
ehl-vah-gohn-day-pah-sah-hay-roh
passenger car

las vías del tren
lahs-vee-ahs-dehl-trehn
train tracks

el furgón de cola
ehl-foor-gohn-day-koh-lah
caboose

el vagón de carga
ehl-vah-gohn-day-kahr-gah
boxcar

Fun Phrases:

el tren	*ehl-trayn*	train
aquí	*ah-**kee***	here
allí	*ah-**yee***	there
veo	***vay**-oh*	I see
ves	*vays*	you see

Challenge:
- If your child is ready, you can teach him how to form a question in Spanish. Simply change the intonation of your voice. Below are some examples:

  ***Ves* una locomotora.** You see an engine.

  ¿*Ves una locomotora*? Do you see an engine?

  Hay dos furgón de colas. There are 2 cabooses.

  ¿Hay dos furgónes de cola? Are there 2 cabooses?

- Remember to teach these lessons as slowly or as quickly as your child needs. If your child is not ready for this challenge, you can always come back to it at a later time.

Actividad Uno

Uh oh, this *tren* is uncoupled! Can you number the pieces of the *tren* to show which order they should be in? When you number a piece, make sure you say the number in Spanish and the name of the train car or engine in Spanish!

Actividad Dos

This little steam engine has lost his whistle. Read this story with your parent's help to see what happens. If he says a word in Spanish, point to it in the picture on the next page.

Once upon a time there was a little steam *locomotora,* who was very sad because he couldn't find his whistle. He traveled along the tracks searching for it. The first thing he saw was a *perro*. He wished he could toot his whistle and say *¡hola!,* but he remembered he had lost his whistle. So, the little steam *locomotora* traveled onward.

Next, the little steam *locomotora* saw something shiny and thought it was his whistle, but it was not. It was his friend the *robot*. He wanted to toot his whistle and say *¡hola!,* but he couldn't, so he continued down the tracks looking for his whistle.

The little steam *locomotora* continued and heard a sound, but it wasn't the right sound. Again, he wanted to toot his whistle to say *¡hola!,* but he couldn't. It was his friend Pedro honking the horn in his *coche*. The little *locomotora* continued on his search for his whistle.

Finally, after searching and searching, the little steam *locomotora* found his whistle. The conductor attached it to the *locomotora* and they went back the way they came from. The steam *locomotora* passed Pedro in his *coche* and he tooted his horn *una* time. Then, he passed his friend the *robot* and tooted his horn *dos* times. Lastly, he passed a *perro* and tooted his horn *tres* times, before heading back to the engine shed for a rest.

Now try to tell the story yourself or make up your own story. Start at the train and follow along the tracks. As you pass each picture, make sure you say their name in Spanish!

Actividad Tres

Hmmmm...a few things are just a bit different, but what? Find the nine differences between the two pictures below. Count the differences in Spanish.

Actividad Cuatro

Make Your Own Cargo Train

What you will need:

shoe box
construction paper
crayons or markers
glue or tape
scissors
string/yarn

What to do:

1. Take the lid off of the shoe box, or cut the top off.
2. Use your imagination and decorate the shoe box to make it look like a train. Attach a string to the end of the train, so you can pull it.
3. Now, you need to take your new train on a delivery trip. Find things you have that you can deliver to your mom or dad. You can tell them what the colors of the items are in Spanish, when you deliver them.

Actividad Cinco

Toys

What you will need:

Some of your toy trains, cars, planes, animals, etc. (You can use anything that we have learned the name of in a previous lesson.)

What to do:

1. Sit down with your mom and dad to play this game.
2. She will say *Tengo*….and then select 1 toy. Then you say *Tienes...* and then the name of the toy.
3. Continue until you both have named all of your toys.

For example:
Your mom might say: *Tengo un coche*
You would reply: *Tienes un coche.*

Vocabulary:

el león *ehl-lay-**ohn***
lion

el elefante
*ehl-ay-lay-**fahn**-tay*
elephant

el oso *ehl-**oh**-soh*
bear

la jirafa *lah-hee-**rah**-fah*
giraffe

la cebra *lah-**say**-brah*
zebra

el tigre *ehl-**tee**-gray*
tiger

el parque zoológico *ehl-pahr-keh-zoh-**loh**-hee-koh*
zoo

Fun Phrases:

pequeño	*pay-**kay**-nyoh*	small
grande	***grahn**-day*	big
lento	***lehn**-toh*	slow
rápido	***rah**-pee-doh*	fast
soy	*soy*	I am
eres	***eh**-rehs*	you are

Teaching Tips:
As you have learned, most adjectives in Spanish go after the noun; however, some adjectives in Spanish go before the noun, such as *pequeño* and *grande*.

el pequeño gato - the little cat

Actividad Uno

Oh no! The animals have escaped from their pens! Can you draw a line between the animals and their correct pens? Remember to say the animal's name in Spanish as you draw the line.

la cebra

el oso

el elefante

50

Actividad Dos

Look at all of the different animals on this page. Some are *grande* and some are very *pequeño*. Using your crayons or markers, draw a *rojo* circle around all of the *grande* animals. Draw a *verde* circle around all of the *pequeño* animals.

Actividad Tres

Uh oh...the animals are all mixed up! Look at each picture and say which parts of each animal make up this new animal. In the empty box, create your own mixed up animal. Then, describe all of the mixed up animals to your parents in Spanish. Remember to use the names of the body parts you have learned!

Actividad Cuatro
Animal Parade

What you will need:
paper plates
crayons
scissors
construction paper
glue

What to do:
1. Create your own animal mask by using the materials listed. You can also make a tail for yourself.
2. Have an animal parade around your house. Make sure you say
   Soy (I am) … to let everyone know which animal you are.
   For example: *Soy un tigre.* (I am a tiger.)

Actividad Cinco
Animal Charades

What you will need:
strips of paper
a cup
a pencil

What to do:
1. Ask your mom or dad to write the names or draw pictures of the animals from this chapter on strips of paper.
2. Fold up the strips of paper and put them in the cup.
3. Take turns with your mom or dad taking a piece of paper from the cup and pretending to be that animal. Try not to make sounds or use words when acting out your animal. Make sure to guess the animal name in Spanish.

Lección 9
Slimy Friends

Vocabulary:

la babosa *lah-bah-**boh**-sah*
slug

la culebra *lah-koo-**lay**-brah*
snake

el caracol
*ehl-kah-rah-**cohl***
snail

la rana *lah-**rah**-nah*
frog

la oruga *lah-oh-**roo**-gah*
caterpillar

Fun Phrases:

me gusta	*meh-**goo**-stah*	I like
te gusta	*teh-**goo**-stah*	you like

Challenge:

You can have your son practice saying things he likes with plural nouns. If a noun is either feminine or masculine the plural for 'the' is *los* if the noun is masculine and *las* if the noun is feminine. Also, if a word ends with a consonant sound, you need to add 'es' to the end of the word to make it plural.

He can practice phrases like:

> *Me gustan las culebras.*   I love the snakes.
> *Me gustan los leones.*   I love the lions.

Actividad Uno

Snakes and Ladders

What you will need:

a die

a counter for each player, for example a small plastic animal or toy car

Vocabulary:

comienzo	*koh-mee-**ehn**-so*	start
fin	*feen*	end

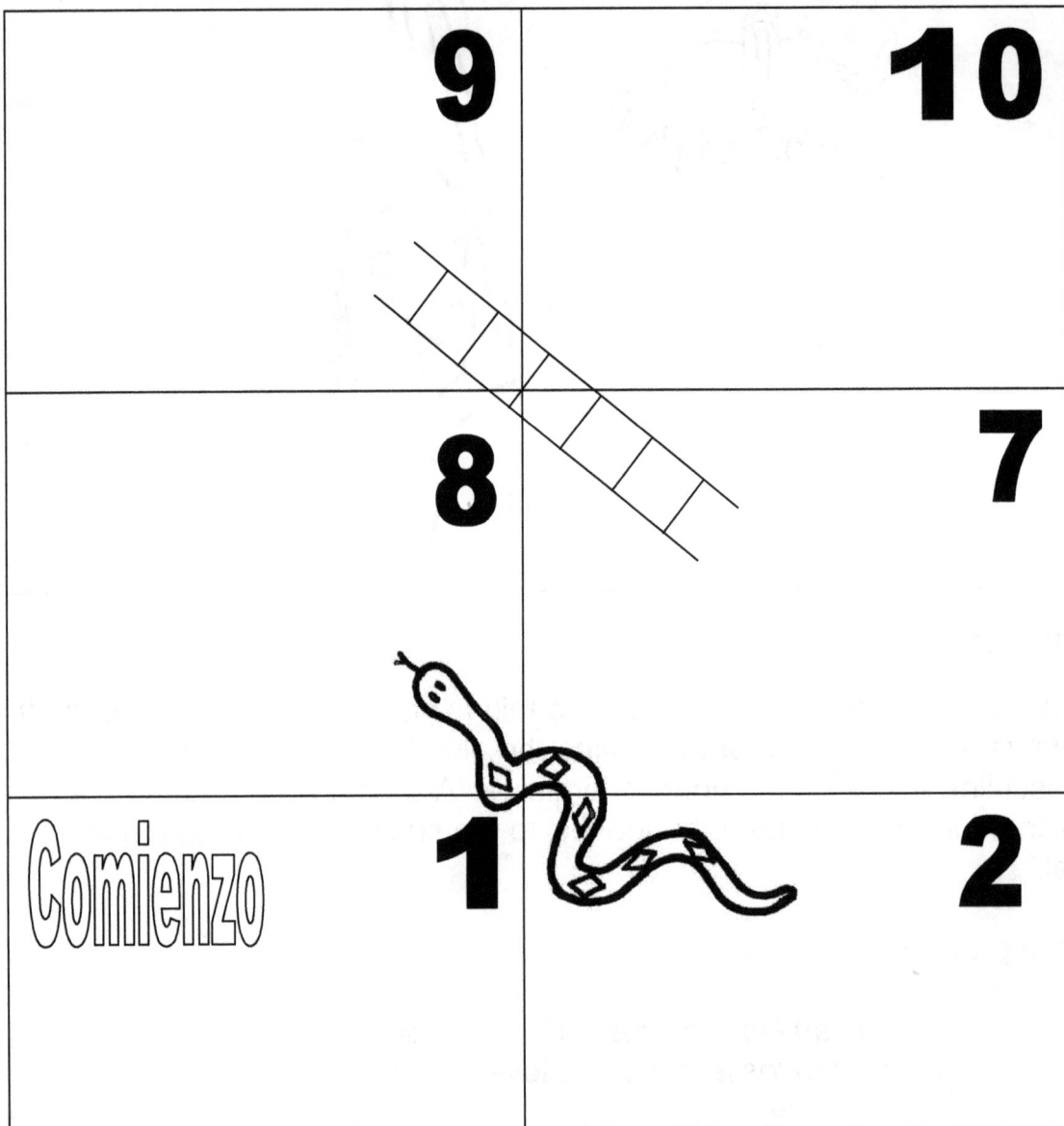

9	10
8	7
Comienzo 1	2

How to Play:

1. The youngest person goes first. Roll the die and then move that many spaces. Count in Spanish as you move your counter.
2. If you land on a *culebra*, you have to slide down it and land on the square at the end of its body.
3. If you land on a ladder, you can climb up to the square it ends on.
4. The first person to reach the finish (*fin*) is the winner!

¡Buena suerte! Good luck!

11	**12** Fin
6	**5**
3	**4**

Actividad Dos

These animals have lost their friends; match each pair of animals and then say their names in Spanish.

Actividad Tres

Pedro wants to go home. As he passes friends on the road, say in Spanish each animal's name and the other things he sees. Say *Veo*…Then, color the picture using the color key below.

color key	
el avión	*negro*
el tigre	*naranja*
el perro	*rojo*
la cebra	*verde*

Actividad Cuatro

Caterpillar Friends

What you will need:

cotton balls
acrylic paint
scissors
paper
glue

What to do:

1. Have your mom or dad help you draw and cut the shape of a caterpillar out of paper.
2. Dip your cotton balls into different colors of paint and let them dry.
3. Glue your cotton balls onto the paper and create a very colorful caterpillar. After you let it dry you can hang it on your fridge. Every time you go to the fridge, point to the different colors and say their names in Spanish.

Actividad Cinco

I Like...

What you will need:

construction paper
crayons

What to do:

1. Take a piece of construction paper and at the top write *me gusta* on it. You can ask your mom or dad to help you.
2. Draw all of the things that *tu gusta*. They could be people, toys, places; anything that *tu gusta*.
3. Show your mom and dad your artwork and tell them all of the things that *tu gusta*.

Lección 10

Rescue Vehicles

Vocabulary:

el carro de remolque
*ehl-**kah**-roh-day-ray-**mohl**-kay*
tow truck

la ambulancia
*lah-ahm-boo-**lahn**-see-ah*
ambulance

el coche de policía
*ehl-**koh**-chay-day-poh-lee-**see**-ah*
police car

el coche de bomberos
*ehl-**koh**-chay-day-bohm-**bay**-rohs*
fire truck

Challenge:

- To create a negative sentence in Spanish, put 'no' before the verb.
  For example:

  I don't see the police car.
  No veo el coche de policía

61

Actividad Uno

My favorite rescue vehicle is *el coche de bomberos*. Which of these rescue vehicles is your favorite? Draw a circle around all of the rescue vehicles you like. As you draw the circle say: '*Me gusta _____*'.

Actividad Dos

Pedro is late for his job at the quarry. Help him follow the path so he can get there as soon as possible. As you pass the different types of vehicles make sure you say their names in Spanish. Also, you can draw your own rescue vehicles on the picture!

Actividad Tres

Pedro needs your help to put out all of the little fires. Color all of the fires *anaranjado* or *rojo* and as you color them count how many fires there are in Spanish. Afterwards, put out the fires by coloring the water *azul* from the hose.

Actividad Cuatro

Memory

You will need:
the memory cards found in the appendix of this book.

What to do:
1. Shuffle the cards.
2. Turn all of the cards upside down in rows in front of you on a table or on the floor.
3. Pick up 2 and see if they match. As you pick up each card, remember to say each picture's name in Spanish. If they match, you can keep those cards and continue with your turn. If they do not match, put them back upside down and then it will be the next player's turn.
4. The player with the most pairs of matched cards wins.

Challenge: You can vary the level of difficulty of this game by using some or all of the pairs of cards.

Actividad Cinco

My Favorite Rescue Vehicle

You will need:
a medium sized box (an old diaper box would work perfectly)
crayons
construction paper
scissors
glue

What to do:
1. Have your mom or dad cut out the bottom and top of the box.
2. Decorate the box as your favorite rescue vehicle.
3. Step inside your rescue vehicle, hold onto the side and off you go!   Remember to say what vehicle you are driving in Spanish as you play in your rescue vehicle. For example: *Soy un coche de policía.*

Appendices

My Spanish Path

Every time you finish a Lección in the book,
color a stone until you reach Pedro.

10 9 8 7 6 5 4 3 2 1

Three cheers for

_____

¡Felicidades!
Congratulations!
You have successfully finished
Spanish for Little Boys.
You did a wonderful job!

English to Spanish Dictionary

a(n)	un/una	*oohn/**ooh**-nah*
airplane	el avión	*ehl-ah-vee-**ohn***
ambulance	la ambulancia	*lah-ahm-boo-**lahn**-see-ah*
and	y	*ee*
ant	la hormiga	*lah-ohr-**mee**-gah*
arm	el brazo	*ehl-**brah**-soh*
bear	el oso	*ehl-**oh**-soh*
bee	la abeja	*lah-ah-**bay**-hah*
bicycle	la bicicleta	*lah-bee-see-**clay**-tah*
big	grande	***grahn**-day*
bird	el pájaro	*ehl-**pah**-hah-roh*
black	negro	***nay**-groh*
blue	azul	*ah-**sool***

box car	el vagón de carga	ehl-vah-**gohn**-day-**kahr**-gah
butterfly	la mariposa	*lah-mah-ree-**poh**-sah*
caboose	el furgón de cola	*ehl-foor-**gohn**-day-**koh**-lah*
car	el coche	*ehl-**koh**-chay*
cat	el gato	*ehl-**gah**-toh*
caterpillar	la oruga	*lah-oh-**roo**-gah*
color	color	*koo-**lohr***
congratulations	felicidades	*feh-lee-cee-**dah**-days*
dog	el perro	*ehl-**pehr**-roh*
eight	ocho	***oh**-choh*
elephant	el elefante	*ehl-ay-lay-**fahn**-tay*
end	fin	*feen*
engine	la locomotora	*lah-loh-koh-moh-**toh**-rah*
fast	rápido	***rah**-pee-doh*

finger	el dedo	*ehl-**day**-doh*
fire truck	el coche de bomberos	*ehl-**koh**-chay-day-bohm-**bay**-rohs*
fish	el pez	*ehl-**pays***
five	cinco	***seen**-koh*
foot	el pie	*ehl-pee-**ay***
four	cuatro	*koo-**aht**-troh*
frog	la rana	*lah-**rah**-nah*
giraffe	la jirafa	*lah-hee-**rah**-fah*
good-bye	adiós	*a-dee-**ohs***
good luck	buena suerte	*boo-**eh**-nah-**swehr**-teh*
green	verde	***vehrr**-day*
hand	la mano	*lah-**mah**-noh*
have a good trip	que tengas un buen viaje	*keh-**tehn**-gahs-oohn-vee-**ah**-hay*
head	la cabeza	*lah-kah-**bay**-sah*

helicopter	el helicóptero	*ehl-ay-lee-**cohp**-tay-roh*
hello	hola	***oh**-la*
here	aquí	*ah-**kee***
hot air balloon	el globo aerostático	*ehl-**gloh**-boh-ah-ay-rohs-**tah**-tee-koh*
how are you?	¿cómo estás?	***koh**-moh-eh-**stahs***
how many?	cuántos	***quahn**-tohs*
I am	soy	*soy*
I have	tengo	***tayn**-goh*
I like	me gusta	*meh-**goo**-stah*
I see	veo	***vay**-oh*
I'm bad	estoy mal	*eh-**stoy**-mahl*
I'm well	estoy bien	*eh-**stoy**-bee-**in***
kite	la cometa	*lah-coh-**may**-tah*
lady bug	la mariquita	*lah-mah-ree-**kee**-tah*

leg	la pierna	*lah-pee-**ehr**-nah*
lesson	lección	*lek-see-**ohn***
lion	el león	*ehl-lay-**ohn***
motorcycle	la motocicleta	*lah-moh-toh-see-**klay**-tah*
my name is	me llamo	*meh-**yah**-moh*
no	no	*noh*
nine	nueve	*noo-**ay**-vay*
one	uno	***oo**-noh*
orange	anaranjado	*ah-nah-rahn-**hah**-doh*
passenger car	el vagón de pasajero	*ehl-vah-**gohn**-day-pah-sah-**hay**-roh*
please	por favor	*pohr-fay-**vohr***
police car	el coche de policía	*ehl-**koh**-chay-day-poh-lee-**see**-ah*
rabbit	el conejo	*ehl-coh-**nay**-hoh*

red	rojo	*roh*-hoh
robot	el robot	*ehl-roh-**boht***
rocket	el cohete	*ehl-coh-**ay**-tay*
see you later	hasta luego	***ahs**-tah-loo-**ay**-goh*
seven	siete	*see-**eh**-tay*
six	seis	***say**-ees*
slow	lento	***lehn**-toh*
slug	la babosa	*lah-bah-**boh**-sah*
small	pequeño	*pay-**kay**-nyoh*
snail	el caracol	*ehl-kah-rah-**cohl***
snake	la culebra	*lah-koo-**lay**-brah*
so-so	así así	*ah-**see**-ah-**see***
spider	la araña	*lah-ah-**rah**-nyah*
start	comienzo	*koh-mee-**ehn**-so*

ten	diez	*dee-**ehs***
tender	la vagoneta	*lah-vah-gohn-**nay**-tah*
thank you	gracias	***grah**-see-ahs*
there	allí	*ah-**yee***
there is/there are	hay	*ah-ee*
three	tres	*trays*
tiger	el tigre	*ehl-**tee**-gray*
toe	el dedo	*ehl-**day**-doh*
tow truck	el carro de remol-que	*ehl-**kah**-roh-day-ray-**mohl**-kay*
train	el tren	*ehl-trayn*
train track	las vías del tren	*lahs-**vee**-ahs-dehl-trehn*
truck	el camión	*ehl-cah-mee-**ohn***
two	dos	*dohs*
what is your name?	¿cómo te llamas?	***koh**-moh-tay-**yah**-mahs*

which	cuál	*koo-**ahl***
white	blanco	***blahn**-koh*
yellow	amarillo	*ah-mah-**ree**-yoh*
you are	eres	***eh**-rehs*
you're welcome	de nada	*day-**nah**-dah*
you have	tienes	*tee-**ehn**-ehs*
you like	te gusta	*teh-**goo**-stah*
you see	ves	*vays*
zebra	la cebra	*lah-**say**-brah*
zoo	el parque zo-ológico	*ehl-**pahr**-keh-zoh-loh-hee-koh*

Spanish to English Dictionary

la abeja	*lah-ah-**bay**-hah*	bee
adiós	*a-dee-**ohs***	good-bye
allí	*ah-**yee***	there
la ambulancia	*lah-ahm-boo-**lahn**-see-ah*	ambulance
amarillo	*ah-mah-**ree**-yoh*	yellow
anaranjado	*ah-nah-rahn-**hah**-doh*	orange
aquí	*ah-**kee***	here
la araña	*lah-ah-**rah**-nyah*	spider
así así	*ah-**see**-ah-**see***	so-so
el avión	*ehl-ah-vee-**ohn***	airplane
azul	*ah-**sool***	blue
la babosa	*lah-bah-**boh**-sah*	slug
la bicicleta	*lah-bee-see-**clay**-tah*	bicycle

blanco	*blahn*-koh	white
el brazo	ehl-*brah*-soh	arm
buena suerte	boo-*eh*-nah-*swehr*-teh	good luck
la cabeza	lah-kah-*bay*-sah	head
el camión	ehl-cah-mee-*ohn*	truck
el caracol	ehl-kah-rah-*cohl*	snail
el carro de remol-que	ehl-*kah*-roh-day-ray-*mohl*-kay	tow truck
la cebra	lah-*say*-brah	zebra
cinco	*seen*-koh	five
el coche	ehl-*koh*-chay	car
el coche de bomberos	ehl-*koh*-chay-day-bohm-*bay*-rohs	fire truck
el coche de po-licía	ehl-*koh*-chay-day-poh-lee-*see*-ah	police car
el cohete	ehl-coh-*ay*-tay	rocket
color	koo-*lohr*	color

la cometa	*lah-coh-**may**-tah*	kite
comienzo	*koh-mee-**ehn**-so*	start
¿cómo estás?	**koh**-*moh-eh-***stahs**	how are you?
¿cómo te llamas?	**koh**-*moh-tay-**yah**-mahs*	what is your name?
el conejo	*ehl-coh-**nay**-hoh*	rabbit
cuál	*koo-**ahl***	which
cuántos	***quahn**-tohs*	how many?
cuatro	*koo-**aht**-troh*	four
la culebra	*lah-koo-**lay**-brah*	snake
de nada	*day-**nah**-dah*	you're welcome
el dedo	*ehl-**day**-doh*	finger/toe
diez	*dee-**ehs***	ten
dos	*dohs*	two

el elefante	*ehl-ay-lay-**fahn**-tay*	elephant
eres	***eh**-rehs*	you are
estoy bien	*eh-**stoy**-bee-**in***	I'm well
estoy mal	*eh-**stoy**-mahl*	I'm bad
felicidades	*feh-lee-cee-**dah**-days*	congratulations
fin	*feen*	end
el furgón de cola	*ehl-foor-**gohn**-day-**koh**-lah*	caboose
el gato	*ehl-**gah**-toh*	cat
el globo aerostático	*ehl-**gloh**-boh-ah-ay-rohs-**tah**-tee-koh*	hot-air balloon
gracias	***grah**-see-ahs*	thank you
grande	***grahn**-day*	big
hasta luego	***ahs**-tah-loo-**ay**-goh*	see you later
hay	*ah-ee*	there is/there are
el helicóptero	*ehl-ay-lee-**cohp**-tay-roh*	helicopter

hola	**oh**-la	hello
la hormiga	lah-ohr-**mee**-gah	ant
la jirafa	lah-hee-**rah**-fah	giraffe
lección	lek-see-**ohn**	lesson
lento	**lehn**-toh	slow
el león	ehl-lay-**ohn**	lion
la locomotora	lah-loh-koh-moh-**toh**-rah	engine
ocho	**oh**-choh	eight
la mano	lah-**mah**-noh	hand
la mariposa	lah-mah-ree-**poh**-sah	butterfly
la mariquita	lah-mah-ree-**kee**-tah	lady bug
me gusta	meh-**goo**-stah	I like
me llamo	meh-**yah**-moh	my name is
la motocicleta	lah-moh-toh-see-**klay**-tah	motocycle

negro	*nay*-groh	black
no	**noh**	no
nueve	noo-**ay**-vay	nine
la oruga	lah-oh-**roo**-gah	caterpillar
el oso	ehl-**oh**-soh	bear
el pájaro	ehl-**pah**-hah-roh	bird
el parque zo-ológico	ehl-**pahr**-keh-zoh-**loh**-hee-koh	zoo
pequeño	pay-**kay**-nyoh	small
el perro	ehl-**pehr**-roh	dog
el pez	ehl-**pays**	fish
el pie	ehl-pee-**ay**	foot
la pierna	lah-pee-**ehr**-nah	leg
por favor	pohr-fay-**vohr**	please
que tengas un buen viaje	keh-**tehn**-gahs-oohn-vee-**ah**-hay	have a good trip

la rana	*lah-**rah**-nah*	frog
rápido	***rah**-pee-doh*	fast
el robot	*ehl-roh-**boht***	robot
rojo	***roh**-hoh*	red
seis	***say**-ees*	six
siete	*see-**eh**-tay*	seven
soy	*soy*	I am
te gusta	*teh-**goo**-stah*	you like
tengo	***tayn**-goh*	I have
tienes	*tee-**ehn**-ehs*	you have
el tigre	*ehl-**tee**-gray*	tiger
el tren	*ehl-trayn*	train
tres	*trays*	three
un/una	*oohn/**ooh**-nah*	a(n)

uno	**oo**-*noh*	one
el vagón de carga	ehl-vah-**gohn**-day-**kahr**-gah	box car
el vagón de pasajero	*ehl-vah-**gohn**-day-pah-sah-**hay**-roh*	passenger car
la vagoneta	*lah-vah-gohn-**nay**-tah*	tender
veo	**vay**-*oh*	I see
verde	**vehrr**-*day*	green
ves	*vays*	you see
las vías del tren	*lahs-**vee**-ahs-dehl-trehn*	train track
y	*ee*	and

Memory Game Cards